SACRED T

The
Guru
Granth
Sahib
and Sikhism

Anita Ganeri

A⁺

Smart Apple Media

Evans Brothers Limited
2A Portman Mansions
Chiltern St.
London W1U 6NR

First published 2003
Text copyright © Anita Ganeri 2003
© in the illustrations Evans Brothers Ltd 2003

Printed in Hong Kong by Wing King Tong Co. Ltd

Editors: Nicola Barber, Louise John
Designer: Simon Borrough
Illustrations: Tracy Fennell, Allied Artists
Production: Jenny Mulvanny
Consultant: Rajinder Singh Panesar

Picture acknowledgements:
Circa Photo Library: p6 (John Smith), p7 (Bipin J
Mistry), p8 (Twin Studio), p11 (Twin Studio), p12
(John Smith), p14, p17 bottom (John Smith), p18
(John Smith), p19 (Bipin J Mistry), p20, p21 (John
Smith)
Hutchison Library: p13 (Liba Taylor)
David Rose: p22 bottom, p24
Peter Sanders: p25
Trip (H Rogers): p9, p10, p15, p16, p17 top, p22 top,
p26, p27

Published in the United States by
Smart Apple Media, 1980 Lookout Drive
North Mankato, Minnesota 56003

Library of Congress Cataloging-in-Publication Data

Ganeri, Anita.
The Guru Granth Sahib and Sikhism / by Anita Ganeri.
p. cm. — (Sacred texts)
Includes index.
Summary: Explains the history and practices of the
religion of Sikhism, especially as revealed through its
sacred book, the Guru Granth Sahib.
Contents: Origins — Structure and contents —
Message and teachings — Study and reading — The
Guru Granth Sahib in daily life.
ISBN 1-58340-245-4
1. ådi-Granth—Criticism and interpretation—Juvenile
literature. 2. Sikhism—Customs and practices—Juvenile
literature. [1. ådi-Granth. 2. Sikhism.] I. Title. II. Sacred
texts (Mankato, Minn.)

BL2017.45.G36 2003
294.6'82—dc21   2003042353

First Edition
9 8 7 6 5 4 3 2 1

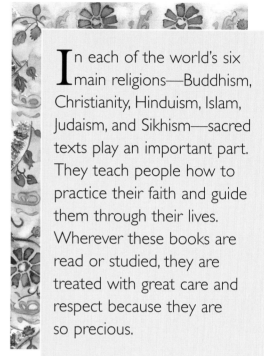

In each of the world's six main religions—Buddhism, Christianity, Hinduism, Islam, Judaism, and Sikhism—sacred texts play an important part. They teach people how to practice their faith and guide them through their lives. Wherever these books are read or studied, they are treated with great care and respect because they are so precious.

The quotations in this book have been translated, and adapted to suit the age range, from the original text of the Guru Granth Sahib.

To Catherine Chambers. A. G.

Contents

Introduction

Origins

Structure and Contents

Message and Teachings

Study and Reading

The Guru Granth Sahib in Daily Life

Introduction

The Sri guru granth Sahib

The Guru Granth Sahib is the sacred book of the Sikhs, who follow the religion of Sikhism. Sikhs believe in one God and try to remember God in everything they do. By living honestly and caring for others, they hope to grow closer to God. Sikhs follow the example set by 10 great teachers, or Gurus. The 10th Sikh Guru, Guru Gobind Singh, died in 1708. He did not name a human Guru to succeed him. Instead, he told the Sikhs that in the future the Guru Granth Sahib was to be their Guru and guide.

How Sikhism began

Sikhism was founded about 500 years ago, in the Punjab region of northwestern India. At that time, the main religions in India were Hinduism and Islam, but there were deep divisions between the two. A holy man called Nanak, who was brought up as a Hindu, introduced a new religion which taught that everyone was equal in God's eyes. He became known as Guru Nanak, the first Sikh Guru.

A Sikh reading from the Guru Granth Sahib, the Sikh sacred text.

The holy book

The Guru Granth Sahib is a collection of hymns and verses written by Guru Nanak and five of the other Sikh Gurus, as well as Hindu and Muslim holy men. The hymns express teachings which Sikhs use as a guide for their lives.

For Sikhs, the Guru Granth Sahib is more than simply a book. They believe that it is the word of God, passed on by the Gurus. Sikhs honor the Guru Granth Sahib as a living Guru and treat it as a precious gift. They often put the title "Sri," or "Sir," before its name, to show respect.

Sikhism today

Today, there are about 14 million Sikhs. Most Sikhs still live in the Punjab region, where Sikhism began, but there are also large Sikh communities in other places, such as North America and Britain. Wherever they live, Sikhs meet in buildings called Gurdwaras to worship and learn more about their faith. Any place can be a Gurdwara, as long as it contains a copy of the Guru Granth Sahib.

"In this dish are placed three things: truth, contentment, and wisdom, as well as the sweetness of God's name, which is the support of everyone. Those who absorb and enjoy it shall be saved. Do not abandon this gift, but always keep it close to your heart."
(GURU GRANTH SAHIB, PAGE 1,430)

The Harimandir, or Golden Temple, in Amritsar, India, is the Sikhs' holiest shrine.

Origins

The first guru

Guru Nanak was born in 1469 in the village of Talwandi, in the Punjab region of northwestern India. His family was Hindu, but Nanak and his father worked for the local Muslim rulers and had many Muslim friends. From an early age, Nanak was deeply religious and spent much of his time meditating and thinking about God.

God calls Guru Nanak

When Nanak was 30 years old, he had an experience that changed his life. One day, he went to the river to bathe, and completely disappeared. His anxious friends and family thought that he must have drowned. Then, three days later, Nanak returned. He told them that God had called him and given him the task of teaching God's message to the world.

Guru Nanak's travels

Guru Nanak spent the rest of his life as a teacher, travelling around India and beyond. He often used poetry to explain his teachings because it was easier for people to remember and learn.

Guru Nanak (center) with the Muslim musician Mardana (left) and Bala (right), a Hindu holy man.

A Muslim musician, called Mardana, often went with him and set his poems to tunes that could be sung easily. A large part of the Guru Granth Sahib is made up of Guru Nanak's poems, or hymns.

What Guru Nanak taught

The first words that Guru Nanak spoke after his calling were: "There is no Hindu, there is no Muslim, so whose path shall I follow? I shall follow God's path." He taught that, in God's eyes, all people are equal, whether they are rich or poor, men or women, or followers of different religions. He also told people to work hard and tell the truth. This story shows his teaching: in one village, Guru Nanak chose to stay at the home of a humble carpenter, Bhai Lalo, rather than with a wealthy merchant, because the carpenter was poor but honest, while the merchant's riches were gained by greed.

Guru Nanak took a piece of bread from Bhai Lalo, the carpenter (left), and from the wealthy merchant (right). When he squeezed both pieces, milk dripped from the carpenter's bread, and blood dripped from the merchant's. This made Guru Nanak's point that the carpenter's humble food was at least earned honestly.

Several stories are told of Guru Nanak's childhood that show that he was special. Once, Nanak fell asleep under a tree when he was meant to be tending the family's buffaloes. The buffaloes wandered off and trampled a farmer's field. But when the farmer went to look, the crops had grown back, better than before.

The later gurus

As Guru Nanak grew older, it became important for him to choose one of his followers to be his successor. One day, he dropped a jug in a muddy ditch and asked his sons to fetch it. They refused because they thought that the Guru's sons were too good to do a job such as that. Instead, a man called Lehna scrambled down after the jug. Lehna became Guru Angad, the second Sikh Guru. "Guru" means "a teacher who helps people to know about God."

The 10 Sikh gurus

1. Guru Nanak (1469–1539)
2. Guru Angad (1504–1552)
3. Guru Amar Das (1479–1574)
4. Guru Ram Das (1534–1581)
5. Guru Arjan (1563–1606)
6. Guru Har Gobind (1595–1644)
7. Guru Har Rai (1630–1661)
8. Guru Har Krishan (1656–1664)
9. Guru Tegh Bahadur (1621–1675)
10. Guru Gobind Singh (1666–1708)

This painting shows the 10 Sikh Gurus.

"Tell me, o wise man, what holds up the sky?
Very fortunate is the person who knows this.
The sun and moon spread their light.
They too show God's presence.
Kabir says, only a person whose mind is filled with God and whose mouth speaks God's name can understand this great truth."

(GURU GRANTH SAHIB, PAGE 329)

Composing the Guru Granth Sahib

There are almost 6,000 hymns in the Guru Granth Sahib, long and short. The hymns were composed by Guru Nanak and five of the other Sikh Gurus—Gurus Angad, Amar Das, Ram Das, Arjan, and Tegh Bahadur. Guru Arjan composed 2,218 hymns; Guru Nanak composed 974 hymns. There are also hymns written by Hindu and Muslim holy men, and the great Indian poet Kabir. These writings are called the bhagat bani. They help to teach Sikhs to respect and be tolerant of other religions.

Guru Gobind Singh

Although he was a great writer and poet, Guru Gobind Singh did not put any of his own hymns into the Guru Granth Sahib. Instead, his hymns were collected together after his death by one of his followers, named Bhai Mani Singh, in a book called the Dasam Granth ("The Book of the 10th Guru"). This is a holy book for Sikhs, and some of its hymns are used in daily prayer. But it is never equal to the Guru Granth Sahib.

Guru Gobind Singh, the 10th Sikh Guru, died in 1708. Before his death, he told the Sikhs that there would be no more human Gurus after him. The Guru Granth Sahib would now be their Guru, and they should look to it for guidance in their faith and in their lives.

Guru Gobind Singh, the 10th and last of the human Gurus of the Sikhs.

Collecting the guru granth Sahib

For many years, Guru Nanak's hymns were not written down. His followers had to learn them and remember them by heart. Later, Guru Nanak and Lehna (Guru Angad) began to collect the hymns together and write them down so that Sikh communities everywhere would have a copy to use. Guru Angad added some of his own hymns, but he always signed them with the name "Nanak." This is because he believed that he was carrying on Guru Nanak's spirit and working on Guru Nanak's behalf, not adding anything new of his own.

Collecting the scriptures

It was the fifth Sikh Guru, Guru Arjan, who collected the hymns together and put them in one sacred book. This was important, to safeguard the original hymns and make sure that their words or messages were not altered. Guru Arjan sent his followers far and wide to collect all the existing versions and bring them to the holy city of Amritsar in India. There, a man named Bhai Gurdas wrote them down, exactly as Guru Arjan told him to. This enormous task took a few years to complete. The collection was called the Adi Granth, which means "first big book."

Sikhs praying in the presence of the Guru Granth Sahib in the Harimandir, or Golden Temple.

A verse by Guru Tegh Bahadur

"The many silent sages lovingly praise the Lord.

Their bodies and minds are purified, as they enshrine the True Lord in their consciousness.

O Nanak, meditate on the Lord, each and every day."

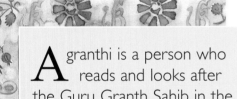

A granthi is a person who reads and looks after the Guru Granth Sahib in the Gurdwara. The first granthi was a very old man named Baba Buddha, who had been a follower of Guru Nanak. He helped to check that the hymns were correct as Bhai Gurdas wrote them down.

A place in the temple

In 1604, Guru Arjan placed the Adi Granth in a specially built temple, called the Harimandir, in Amritsar. It was placed on a raised throne under a canopy. Guru Arjan bowed down in front of it and told the other Sikhs to do the same. In this way, they were showing respect for the scriptures that would guide them throughout their lives. (You can read more about how Sikhs honor the Adi Granth on pages 20 and 21.)

The Guru Granth Sahib

One hundred years later, Guru Gobind Singh added the hymns of his father, Guru Tegh Bahadur, to the Adi Granth. After his death, this new version became known as the Guru Granth Sahib. The Indian word *Sahib* means "lord" or "master." This is the version that Sikhs all over the world use today. The original copy of the Adi Granth still survives. It is kept in a town called Kartarpur, in the Punjab.

A granthi may be a man or woman because, for Sikhs, everyone is equal.

From the guru's mouth

Early copies of the Guru Granth Sahib were written out by hand. To copy them was a great honor, but each copy took many months to complete. Today, modern printing presses mean that thousands of copies can be printed. Each printed copy of the Guru Granth Sahib has 1,430 pages and is identical. So, if one turns to page 100 or page 1,430 in any copy, he or she will find the same words written on the page.

The order of the hymns

The thousands of hymns in the Guru Granth Sahib are not arranged by author or subject. They are divided into 31 musical melodies, called ragas, to which they are sung. Some ragas are happy; others are sad. Under each raga, the hymns are arranged by author, in the order in which they were written. The hymns of Guru Nanak come first, followed by those of the other Gurus, then the hymns of the other holy men. At the beginning and end of the Guru Granth Sahib, there are prayers which Sikhs use in daily worship. These are meant to be recited, not sung.

Set to music

The whole of the Guru Granth Sahib is written in poetry, and most of the hymns are meant to be sung. In the

The musicians who accompany the singing of hymns in the Gurdwara are called ragis. They play instruments such as tablas (Indian drums) and the harmonium. The musician, Mardana, who travelled with Guru Nanak, played an ancient Indian instrument called a rabab. It was like a guitar with four strings. It was played by plucking the strings.

Gurdwara, worshippers sing the hymns in a slow and steady way so that they can understand the message of the words. This singing of hymns to music is called kirtan. It is a very important part of Sikh worship.

Sikh musicians in the Gurdwara.

From the guru's mouth

The Guru Granth Sahib is written in a script called gurmukhi, which means "from the Guru's mouth." It was developed by Guru Angad for writing down Punjabi, the language which Guru Nanak spoke. Today, Sikh children learn to read gurmukhi at home or in classes held in the Gurdwara. Translations of the Guru Granth Sahib into other languages are allowed to help non-Punjabi speakers. But only copies in the original language are used for services and ceremonies.

"Sing god's praise, hear it sung, and let your heart be filled with love. god will bring peace to your home and take away all your sadness."
(GURU GRANTH SAHIB, PAGE 2)

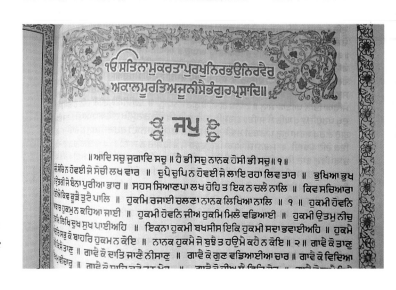

The Guru Granth Sahib is written in gurmukhi script. This picture shows the opening page.

Message and Teachings

What the Guru Granth Sahib teaches

The writings of the Guru Granth Sahib are called gurbani, which means "the word of the Guru." Sikhs believe that they are the word of God, passed on by the Gurus. The hymns of the Guru Granth Sahib praise God and tell Sikhs what God is like. By reading or listening to the holy book, Sikhs believe that God is speaking to them.

About God

Sikhs believe that there is one God, who created the universe and everything in it. God is always present, and sees and knows everything. God is all-powerful, was not born, and will not die. Sikhs do not talk about God as male or female, but often use the name Waheguru, meaning "Wonderful Lord." The Mool Mantar (below) sums up what Sikhs believe about God and begins the Guru Granth Sahib.

Sikhs showing respect to the Guru Granth Sahib. They believe that God speaks to them through their holy book.

"There is only one God
Whose name is Truth
God the creator
is without fear
is without hate
is timeless and without shape
is beyond death, the enlightened ones,
and is understood through God's grace."

(MOOL MANTAR, GURU GRANTH SAHIB, PAGE 1)

The Ik onkar symbol.

About equality

Sikhs believe that everyone is equal, because God created all human beings. No one is more important or better than anyone else. In Guru Nanak's time, women were often considered to be inferior to men and were treated badly. Guru Nanak taught that men and women are equal. He also taught Sikhs to respect everyone, rich or poor, and whatever religion they follow.

Sharing langar

After a service in a Gurdwara, the Sikh place of worship, Sikhs share a special meal called langar. All the members of the Gurdwara help to prepare and serve the meal. Everyone is welcome to share langar, including people who are not Sikhs. This is an important way of expressing the Sikh belief that everyone is equal.

A Sikh woman serving out langar in the Gurdwara.

Service and salvation

The Guru Granth Sahib contains the main teachings of Sikhism. For Sikhs, it is their guide through life, and it gives them rules and advice for loving God and living good lives. One of these rules is that Sikhs should remember God by reading and thinking about the teachings of the Gurus, as written in the Guru Granth Sahib.

Two young Sikh girls say their evening prayers.

Serving others

The Guru Granth Sahib teaches Sikhs to serve and care for other people. Serving or helping others is a very important Sikh belief, called sewa. Sikhs believe that helping other people is a way of worshipping and becoming closer to God. Sewa might mean devoting time to help someone, looking after someone who is sick, or giving money to the poor. Sewa may also mean doing work in the Gurdwara, such as cleaning, doing repairs, or helping to prepare langar.

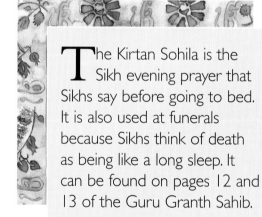

The Kirtan Sohila is the Sikh evening prayer that Sikhs say before going to bed. It is also used at funerals because Sikhs think of death as being like a long sleep. It can be found on pages 12 and 13 of the Guru Granth Sahib.

> "We are gathered to worship and praise God and ponder on God's name. Sing the glory, reflect on the wonders of the One who is ruler and protector of all things."
>
> (Kirtan Sohila, Guru Granth Sahib, pages 12–13)

The story of Bhai Kanhaya

This story shows the importance of sewa. Once, in the time of Guru Gobind Singh, a terrible battle took place between the Sikhs and Muslims. The battle lasted for several days, and many men were wounded on both sides. A kind-hearted Sikh named Bhai Kanhaya took water to the wounded and dying. Some Sikh soldiers complained to the Guru that Bhai Kanhaya had helped the enemy. Bhai Kanhaya replied that he saw no Muslims nor Sikhs, only God's people. Guru Gobind Singh praised Bhai Kanhaya for acting like a true Sikh and helping those in need.

Sikhs clearing away the dishes after the langar.

Seeking salvation

The Guru Granth Sahib contains many teachings about life after death. Sikhs believe that when they die, their souls are reborn in other bodies. This depends on their past actions, good and bad, and on God's grace. If people worship God and follow the teachings of the Gurus, then God will set them free to be with Him. This is called mukti, or salvation. To reach mukti, a Sikh must be "gurmukh," which means "filled with God."

Study and Reading

Reading and respecting the Guru Granth Sahib

The Guru Granth Sahib is always treated with great care because it is regarded as the word of God. It is given the same respect and honor that Sikhs would show to a human guru.

In the Gurdwara

The Guru Granth Sahib on its throne in the Gurdwara.

The place where Sikhs meet for worship is called a Gurdwara, which means "the door of the Guru." Inside the prayer room of a Gurdwara, the Guru Granth Sahib is placed on a raised platform or throne, called a Takht, under a beautifully carved canopy. This is the sort of throne that a human guru would sit on. A Sikh is chosen to read from the Guru Granth Sahib. He or she is called a granthi. The granthi waves a fan, called a chauri, over the Guru Granth Sahib. This is the sort of fan that used to be waved over Gurus to shield them from the sun. The presence of the Guru Granth Sahib turns any building into a Gurdwara.

Showing respect

Before Sikhs visit the Gurdwara, they take a bath or wash. In the Gurdwara, they take off their shoes and cover their heads to show respect. In the prayer room, they walk towards the Guru Granth Sahib, and bow or kneel in front of it. They also leave an offering of money or food. Everyone sits cross-legged on the floor, to show that they are all equal. As they sit down, they take care not to turn their backs toward the Guru Granth Sahib.

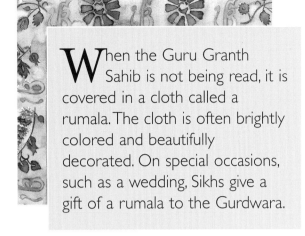

When the Guru Granth Sahib is not being read, it is covered in a cloth called a rumala. The cloth is often brightly colored and beautifully decorated. On special occasions, such as a wedding, Sikhs give a gift of a rumala to the Gurdwara.

A night's rest

At night, the Guru Granth Sahib is closed, wrapped in cloths, and taken from the prayer room. It is put in a room of its own overnight. A ceremony is held to "put it to bed," and another is held to return it to the prayer room in the morning. It is carried on a person's head, which is a great honor for the person. This special room is called Sach Khand Sahib, which means "the realm of truth."

The Guru Granth Sahib is respected so much that it is covered with a rumala cloth.

This prayer is sung when a copy of the Guru Granth Sahib is placed in a home or Gurdwara:

"Blessed is the hour when I see you.
I am glad to be in your presence.
You are the giver of life, my beloved God;
I maintain my whole being by keeping you in mind.
Your teaching is true, your word is sweet,
Your eyes see everything, you are calmness itself.
Your patience is the source of my peace,
Your law is unchanging, my Sovereign.
My God is beyond birth and death."

(GURU GRANTH SAHIB, PAGE 562)

The Guru Granth Sahib in Daily Life

The Guru Granth Sahib in daily life

The Guru Granth Sahib is read as part of a Sikh's daily life, both at home and at services in the Gurdwara. Sikhs believe that God speaks to them through the holy book. The Guru Granth Sahib is used for prayers and guidance, and consulted for advice and comfort in everyday life and at times of need, such as when a loved one dies.

A gutka, or Sikh prayer book, used daily by Sikhs.

At home

Many Sikhs have a copy of the Guru Granth Sahib at home. They treat it as an honored guest and, if possible, keep it in a special room of its own. This room becomes a Gurdwara because the Guru Granth Sahib is kept there. The oldest person in the family takes care of the holy book, and opens it in the morning and reads the morning prayer. Family members offer their respects to the Guru Granth Sahib before they set off for school or work. In the evening, they sit before it and listen to a reading from the text. Sikhs also have smaller books, called gutkas, which contain their daily prayers.

ਜਪੁ ਜੀ ਸਾਹਿਬ

ੴ ਸਤਿਨਾਮੁ ਕਰਤਾ ਪੁਰਖੁ
ਨਿਰਭਉ ਨਿਰਵੈਰੁ
ਅਕਾਲ ਮੂਰਤਿ ਅਜੂਨੀ ਸੈਭੰ
ਗੁਰਪ੍ਰਸਾਦਿ ॥
ਜਪੁ ॥
ਆਦਿ ਸਚੁ ਜੁਗਾਦਿ ਸਚੁ ॥
ਹੈ ਭੀ ਸਚੁ
ਨਾਨਕ ਹੋਸੀ ਭੀ ਸਚੁ ॥੧॥
ਸੋਚੈ ਸੋਚਿ ਨ ਹੋਵਈ ਜੇ ਸੋਚੀ ਲਖ
ਵਾਰ ॥ ਚੁਪੈ ਚੁਪਿ ਨ ਹੋਵਈ ਜੇ ਲਾਇ
ਰਹਾ ਲਿਵ ਤਾਰ ॥ ਭੁਖਿਆ ਭੁਖ ਨ
ਉਤਰੀ ਜੇ ਬੰਨਾ ਪੁਰੀਆ ਭਾਰ ॥ਸਹਸ

Daily guidance

Most of the prayers that Sikhs use at home and
in the Gurdwara come from the Guru Granth
Sahib. The morning prayer is called the Japji
Sahib, and was composed by Guru Nanak.
It reminds Sikhs of God's greatness and that
they should remember God in the day ahead.
The words of another Sikh prayer, called the
Sukhmani Sahib, are also given on the right.

Amrit ceremony

When young Sikhs join the Khalsa, or Sikh
family, a special ceremony is held in the
Gurdwara in the presence of the Guru Granth
Sahib. The people who are about to enter the
Khalsa bathe and put on clean clothes. They must
also wear special symbols as signs of their faith.
During the ceremony, they are given amrit (a
mixture of sugar and water, prepared while
reciting five special prayers), and they promise to
follow the Gurus' teachings. There are prayers and
readings from the Guru Granth Sahib, including
the Japji Sahib.

*Sikhs preparing amrit for the
special amrit ceremony.*

"Turn to God in
contemplation. In
calling God to mind,
find peace. Thus our
inner troubles are
stilled, and all
anguish is driven
away."

(SUKHMANI PRAYER, GURU
GRANTH SAHIB, PAGE 262)

After a service in the
Gurdwara, the granthi
opens the Guru Granth
Sahib at random and reads
aloud the first verse on the
left-hand page. This verse is
called a vak, or hukam. It
gives the Guru's message, or
guidance, for the day.

Rites of passage

The most important times in a Sikh's life are marked by special ceremonies. These all take place in front of the Guru Granth Sahib.

Naming ceremony

Soon after a baby is born, the words of the Mool Mantar (see page 16) are whispered in its ear. A few weeks later, the parents take the baby to the Gurdwara to choose a name. The granthi opens the Guru Granth Sahib at random and reads the first word on the left-hand page. The parents choose a name for their baby which begins with the first letter of that word. Then the granthi announces the name to the congregation. The congregation replies, "Sat sri akal," which means, "God is truth."

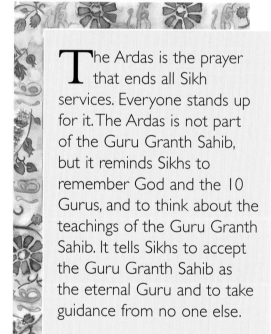

The Ardas is the prayer that ends all Sikh services. Everyone stands up for it. The Ardas is not part of the Guru Granth Sahib, but it reminds Sikhs to remember God and the 10 Gurus, and to think about the teachings of the Guru Granth Sahib. It tells Sikhs to accept the Guru Granth Sahib as the eternal Guru and to take guidance from no one else.

Sikh weddings

Sikh weddings may be held in the Gurdwara or at home, but they must take place in front of the Guru Granth Sahib. In the Gurdwara, the bride and groom sit facing the Guru Granth Sahib.

The ceremony begins with hymns and prayers from the holy book, and a talk about what marriage means. The most important part of the ceremony is the Lavan hymn, composed by Guru Ram Das for his own daughter's wedding (the first verse appears below). As each of the four verses is sung, the bride and groom walk around the Guru Granth Sahib four times to seal their marriage.

Sikh weddings take place in front of the Guru Granth Sahib.

"In this first circle, God has shown you the duties of family life. Accept the Guru's word as your guide, and it will make you free from sin. Meditate on the Name of God, which is the theme of all the scriptures. Devote yourself to God, and all evil will go away. Blessed are those who hold God in their hearts. They are always happy and content."

(LAVAN HYMN, GURU GRANTH SAHIB, PAGE 773)

Funeral prayers

When a Sikh dies, people sing hymns and read from the Guru Granth Sahib to comfort the person's family. Then the body is put in a coffin and taken to the Gurdwara. The coffin is placed facing the Guru Granth Sahib. After the funeral service, the body is taken for cremation. At this sad time, some families arrange for relatives and friends to read the Guru Granth Sahib right through, at home. This period of mourning lasts from 10 to 14 days.

Sikh festivals

During the year, the Guru Granth Sahib is read at Sikh festivals called gurpurbs. A gurpurb is a holy day in honor of the Gurus. These festivals mark the birthdays and deaths of the Gurus. On these special occasions, the whole of the Guru Granth Sahib is read aloud, non-stop, and the holy book is carried in a procession through the streets.

The place where Guru Gobind Singh revised the Adi Granth is called Takht Damdama Sahib. It is in the Punjab (see page 13). This place was declared to be the religious school of the Sikhs. Many Sikhs go there to learn how to read the Guru Granth Sahib so that they can serve as granthis. Religious material produced there is thought to be the most authentic.

The gurus' birthdays

Sikhs celebrate Guru Nanak's birthday in October or November, and Guru Gobind Singh's birthday in December or January. In many places, there are joyful processions through the streets, led by five Sikhs who represent the first five members of the Khalsa. Next comes the Guru Granth Sahib on its throne. It is carried on a truck or float and decorated with banners and flowers. People follow the float and sing hymns from the Guru Granth Sahib. They may also give sweets or fruits to onlookers.

A Sikh street procession to celebrate the birthday of Guru Nanak.

The death of Guru Arjan

Sisganj, the site of the martyrdom of Guru Tegh Bahadur.

In June, a gurpurb is held to remember the death of Guru Arjan. This is one of the most important events in Sikh history. In Guru Arjan's time, the Mughals, who were Muslims, ruled India. The Mughal emperor, Jahangir, was suspicious of Guru Arjan and disliked the fact that the Sikh religion had become so popular. He arrested Guru Arjan and put him in prison. Guru Arjan was tortured and killed because he refused to give up his religion. He became the first Sikh martyr (someone who dies for his faith). Another gurpurb is held in November or December to remember the death of another Sikh martyr, Guru Tegh Bahadur.

Akhand path

The most important part of a gurpurb is a reading of the Guru Granth Sahib in the Gurdwara. It is read from beginning to end, without stopping, which takes about 48 hours. This is called an akhand path. A team of Sikhs takes turns to read, for no longer than two hours at a time. There is also a reserve reader, in case someone is taken ill. The reading is timed to end early in the morning of the festival day. Worshippers can come to the Gurdwara to listen for several hours at a time.

"When a lamp is lit, darkness is dispelled. Likewise, by reading religious books, the darkness of the mind is destroyed."
(GURU GRANTH SAHIB, PAGE 791)

glossary

Adi Granth Another name for the Guru Granth Sahib. Adi Granth means "first book."

Akhand path A non-stop reading of the Guru Granth Sahib on festivals and other special occasions.

Amrit A mixture of sugar and water, used at many Sikh ceremonies. Amrit is thought to have healing properties and to give everlasting life.

Amrit vela The hour before dawn, which is believed to be especially precious for prayer.

Ardas A very important Sikh prayer that remembers God, the 10 Gurus, and the Sikh faith. It is said at the end of services in the Gurdwara.

Bhagat bani The hymns in the Guru Granth written by Sikh, Hindu, and Muslim holy men—not Gurus.

Chauri A fan or whisk that is waved over the Guru Granth Sahib during worship as a sign of respect.

Dasam Granth A collection of hymns written by Guru Gobind Singh. Dasam Sahib means "10th book," or "the book of the 10th Guru."

Granthi A devout Sikh appointed by the Gurdwara to read from the Guru Granth Sahib.

Gurbani The writings of the Sikh Gurus and other holy men in the Guru Granth Sahib. Gurbani means "word of the Guru."

Gurdwara A building where Sikhs meet for worship. Any place can be a Gurdwara, as long as it has a copy of the Guru Granth Sahib. Gurdwara means "gateway of the Guru."

Gurmukhi The script in which the Guru Granth Sahib is written. Gurmukhi means "from the Guru's mouth."

Gurpurb A Sikh festival to remember the birth, death, or another event in the life of one of the Sikh Gurus.

Guru In Indian religions, a guru is a teacher or spiritual guide.

Guru Amar Das The third Sikh Guru, who lived from 1479 to 1574.

Guru Angad The second Sikh Guru, who lived from 1504 to 1552.

Guru Arjan The fifth Sikh Guru, who lived from 1563 to 1606.

Guru Gobind Singh The 10th Sikh Guru, who lived from 1666 to 1708. Before he died, he named the Guru Granth Sahib as his successor.

Guru Granth Sahib The holy book of the Sikhs. It is also called the Adi Granth.

Guru Har Gobind The sixth Sikh Guru, who lived from 1595 to 1644.

Guru Har Krishan The eighth Sikh Guru, who lived from 1656 to 1664.

Guru Har Rai The seventh Sikh Guru, who lived from 1630 to 1661.

Guru Nanak The first Sikh Guru, who lived from 1469 to 1539.

Guru Ram Das The fourth Sikh Guru, who lived from 1534 to 1581.

Guru Tegh Bahadur The ninth Sikh Guru, who lived from 1621 to 1675.

Gutka A small book that contains the daily prayers used by Sikhs. It is kept on a shelf, wrapped in cloth, to show respect.

Harimandir Another name for the Golden Temple, in Amritsar, India. Harimandir means "temple of God." This is the holiest place for Sikhs.

Hymn A religious song which praises or thanks God.

Ik onkar A Sikh symbol that is made up of the letters that mean "There is only one God."

Japji Sahib The Sikh morning prayer which was composed by Guru Nanak.

Khalsa The Sikh family or brotherhood. Many Sikhs join the Khalsa at a special ceremony in the Gurdwara.

Kirtan Hymns sung to music as part of a Sikh service.

Kirtan Sohila The evening prayer that Sikhs say before they go to bed. It is also used at funerals.

Langar The meal that everyone can share after a service in the Gurdwara. The Gurdwara's kitchen or dining hall is also called langar. Langar means "anchor."

Mool Mantar The opening verses of the Guru Granth Sahib, recited by Sikhs as part of their worship.

Mukti This word means "being freed from being born again and again."

Raga Musical tunes to which the hymns in the Guru Granth Sahib are supposed to be sung.

Ragi Musicians who play instruments to accompany the singing of hymns in the Gurdwara.

Rumala A beautifully decorated cloth used to cover the Guru Granth Sahib.

Sach khand sahib The "realm of truth," where a person becomes one with God. It is sometimes called heaven.

Sewa The Sikh idea of service, which means helping other people.

Sukhmani sahib The Sikh hymn of peace, composed by Guru Arjan. It is read every day in morning worship.

Takht Five great Sikh shrines in India where decisions affecting the Sikh religion are made. Takht means "throne."

Vak The verse read aloud every day when the Guru Granth Sahib is opened at random. It is also called hukam.

Waheguru The name that Sikhs use for God. Waheguru means "wonderful God."

Index